Plants in My World

WHAT GROWS IN AN ORCHARD?

Elise Collier

NEW YORK

Published in 2018 by The Rosen Publishing Group, Inc.
29 East 21st Street, New York, NY 10010

First Edition

Editor: Theresa Morlock
Book Design: Michael Flynn

Photo Credits: Cover apiguide/Shutterstock.com; p. 5 Jason Loucas/Getty Images; p. 6 Iakov Filimonov/Shutterstock.com; p. 9 Fineart1/Shutterstock; p. 10 kram9/Shutterstock.com; p. 10 (inset) Joanna Stankiewicz/Shutterstock; p. 13 John Block/Getty Images; p. 14 E.J. Johnson/Shutterstock.com; p. 17 rommma/Shutterstock.com; p. 18 NataSnow/Shutterstock.com; p. 21 KidStock/Getty Images; p. 22 BJI / Blue Jeans Images.

Cataloging-in-Publication Data

Names: Collier, Elise.
Title: What grows in an orchard? / Elise Collier.
Description: New York : PowerKids Press, 2018. | Series: Plants in my world | Includes index.
Identifiers: ISBN 9781508161592 (pbk.) | ISBN 9781508161615 (library bound) | ISBN 9781508161608 (6 pack)
Subjects: LCSH: Orchards–Juvenile literature. | Fruit trees–Juvenile literature.
Classification: LCC SB357.2 C6398 2018 | DDC 634–dc23

Manufactured in China

CPSIA Compliance Information: Batch #BS17PK: For Further Information contact Rosen Publishing, New York, New York at 1-800-237-9932

Please visit: www.rosenpublishing.com and www.habausa.com

CONTENTS

What's an Orchard?

An orchard is a place where fruit trees grow. Apples, cherries, pears, and oranges are just a few fruits that grow in orchards. Nut trees grow in orchards, too.

How Trees Grow

A farmer plants the trees and helps them grow. Farmers grow trees so they can sell the fruit. Growing an orchard is hard work.

Sometimes trees need dead branches cut off. This is called pruning. A farmer uses big cutters called pruning shears. The shears snap off dead branches.

An orchard needs healthy soil. One way to make soil healthy is to add compost. Compost is made from scraps of old food. Rotten food turns into good soil.

Squirrels and birds try to eat the fruit in orchards. Some farmers keep a barn cat to scare away these pests. Barn cats chase away critters that try to steal orchard fruits.

13

Picking Fruit

When fruit is ripe, it is ready to be picked! Collecting fruit is called harvesting. The amount of fruit that's picked is measured by the bushel. A bushel is a big basket full of fruit.

Apples and pears can be picked in the fall. Cherries and peaches are ripe in the summer. The time when fruit is ripe is known as the harvest season.

Families visit orchards to spend time together and have fun. They collect as much fruit as they can and bring it home.

Eating the Harvest

There are so many ways to eat tasty fruit! Apples can also be made into applesauce. Some farmers use a press to turn apples into cider.

Fruit helps our bodies stay healthy and strong. You can visit an orchard to see where your fruit comes from. An orchard is a great place to spend a day with your family.

WORDS TO KNOW

bushel

shears

soil

INDEX